Praise for
Border Duende

In this evocative collection of poems, *Border Duende*, Gina Valdés
explores the complex intersections of cultural identity, gender, and
politics through the lens of the Mexican-American experience.
"The border is a wall of barbed lies," she says, giving us a hint on
how to read her book. Drawing on childhood memories, family
history, and current events, Valdés weaves together a tapestry that
is both raw and nuanced. With a powerful voice that resonates
long after the final page, Valdés cements her place as a vital voice
in contemporary Chicano literature.

—**Agustín Cadena**, author of more than
thirty volumes of poetry, fiction, & essays

There is a deceptive simplicity in Gina Valdés' poems that opens
the reader's heart to their gift of singular wide-angled perspective.
Border Duende flows with a tenacious capacity for humor and for
tender and deep-rooted compassion—that earthen pot of poetry.
The cultural textures these poems offer are rooted in a simple
clarity of the validity of variation and the subtle balancing of
tensions. The poetic voice as keen observer juxtaposes and shifts
kaleidoscopically, speaks for an array of joys, slits, and wounds, for
the seeds of light and love, for a geography of cultural crossroads
that document the subtle threads of merging. Border Duende
brings the reader to the very borders of the poetic, of human life:

"On my walk on earth / may I walk on earth's edge / sky's rim / where worlds meet."

With her duende as guide in her book *Border Duende*, Gina Valdés takes us on a journey through a land of "contacts and fractures," of deserts, walls, and rivers, where Chaplin and Cantinflas romp and "El Santo wrestles Batman." Engaging language as inventive as the border itself, each poem is a portrayal of life along this international line. She writes, "words followed me home," the result of that original enchantment is a delicious volume of poetry written "under the spell of two tongues."

Border Duende

FLOWERSONG
PRESS

poetry by
Gina Valdés

FLOWERSONG
PRESS

To the memory of my parents
George R. Valdés and Mary Escobar
and my sister Martha H. Valdés.

Winner of the
Américo Paredes Literary Awards
Prize for Poetry

PRICKLY PEAR PUBLISHING
& NOPALLI PRESS

table of contents

1.

2

3

4

1.

Acts of Protest

She didn't turn in the womb,
come out head first in accordance with
biological laws: her first non-conformist act.

Instead she exposed to the world
her buttocks: her second act of protest.

And refused to cry: her third defiant act.

The doctor acted quickly with slaps
until she let out a loud wail

rattling the walls
of the segregated hospital
in the race-rioting city,

wails merging with black-out sirens
of a world at war,

clashing with her father
expecting a son.

At birth, poised for a life of resistance,
testing the power of clamor,

primed to traverse walls.

Heroes

All my tíos went
off to war. Tender-
hearted draftees: Rodolfo,
too flat-footed to walk
to the front, ended up
peeling one-hundred-pound sacks
of potatoes, cooking,
armed with salt, oil,
and spices, fighting against
soldiers' growling
stomachs, homesickness.

The others: Ernesto, Gaspar,
Jimmy, marched
to the front, with the stars
and stripes over their hearts.

All but one,
Luis, the renegade
with fast feet, perfect vision,
went A.W.O.L, refused
to be cannon fodder.

All my tías, waiting
for heroes, welcomed all of them
back home.

Héroes

Todos mis tíos se fueron
a la guerra. Conscriptos
de tiernos corazones.
Rodolfo, pies demasiado planos
para caminar al frente, terminó
pelando bolsas de cien libras
de papas, cocinando, armado
de sal, aceite y especias, luchando
contra estómagos vacíos
y la nostalgia del soldado.

Los otros, Ernesto,
Gaspar y Jimmy, marcharon
al frente, con las estrellas
y las franjas sobre el pecho.

Todos menos uno,
Luis, el renegado,
de pies ligeros, visión perfecta,
desertó, se negó a ser
carne de cañón.

Todas mis tías, a la espera
de héroes, celebraron
la vuelta de todos a casa.

Our Home

Papá tried to ignore
the signs staked in lawns,
stood smiling at doors .
slamming on his dark face.

Mamá with the smooth
alabaster skin
of a 40's Hollywood star
rented the houses we lived in.

Race riots in Los Angeles.
War abroad. *Why join
an army waging war on you,*
abuela said.

Papá wavered, decided to go,
with his U.S.-born family,
back to Mexico. He, destined
to never return to the States.

But we, his daughters,
came north again,

to uproot the signs,
to reclaim our home.

The Gift

In a wide-lined tablet appeared
simple geometric forms that bent,
diversified, gained sound, my hand
guided by the steady hand of
la maestra Cuca. Cuquita.

With each new musical letter
my eyes grew wider, prompting
a boy to say, *You look like an owl.*

When the letters assembled
into my name, I scanned the room
for applause, saw thirty busy hands,
pocked desks and blackboard,
floor and walls giving off disinfectant,
a jar with a green shoot pushing
through cotton.

Words followed me home, found
paper to dance on, linked into poems
inspired by poems in yellowing pages
of abuela's books.

In our kitchen, I embraced
a large pumpkin destined for syrupy
pulp floating in milk

and dashed out, the globe carrying me
to Cuquita's house.

It landed on her porch, back from carriage
to pumpkin. I knocked until before me
stood her half-blind sister with sunglasses.

I lifted and offered the autumn fruit--
cucurbita pepo—for Cuquita who
gave me words, names, stories, poems:
the alphabet cornucopia.

Little Explosions

I feared her before that lab
of bubbling colored tubes, setting off
little explosions:

the chemistry set she demanded
for her ninth Christmas.

Tomboy, they called her,
mamá and tías laughing at
her tagging along with papá
to the barbershop.

I didn't expect what boiled over,
the fevered shriek of my friend's
mother warning her: *Never
ever play with her marimacho sister,*

the weighted words brass knuckles
landing on my stomach.

From a distance I watched her
transfixed by the fuming lab,

spied her wrestling
teasing neighbor boys,

learned to dodge
her warrior hands,

knew mamá, papá, and tías
couldn't protect me
or her.

Six and speed-learning
we were on our own,
all around us chemicals bubbling.

Border Duende

This is a mystery I may never solve,
unless a border duende whispers the truth
and I wake to hear it.

Mamá (who worships the god of secrets)
will never tell what truly happened that night.

The air crackled with positive ions
that day in Ensenada: birds hopped
on electrical currents crisscrossing the sky,
uncombed cats slinked through streets,
curtains parted and closed.

Papá cornered me, the youngest, alone
in our yard. Was I staying or leaving?
Where was I going? When?

Papá was building a house of cedar
and sons, uninterested in daughters.
His moneyed sister fancied a family
with his three girls.

The evening sun sparked the sky red
and four plastic bags leaned near our door.
A woman in an old car cruised our unpaved street
scouting for our nonexistent house number.

All mamá will tell: we fled at midnight
in a Ford steered by the aging American lover
of her young brother.

What a border duende reveals:
a hushed summer night
scented by sea breeze and laurel,
a lime slice of moon, a border guard falling
under the spell of mamá's sad beauty;

on the eyelids of slumbering daughters,
the flutter and glimmer of dreams.
All three, nine, twelve, and fifteen,
asleep in the back seat of a beat-up Ford
in the defining event of our lives.

What potent powder did mamá stir
into our evening's café con leche,
fearful that one or all
might choose papá or wealth.

She will remain eerily silent, like the night
of our momentous crossing.

And we crossed with wings;
our U.S. birth certificates hiding
in the darkness of mamá's purse.

Who needs papers in a charmed world?

when earth, moon, stars, wind, ocean, hills,
a one-eyed jalopy, a lovesick Americana,
and a moonstruck guard conspire
to help: to answer a woman's silent cry.

The Double

I return to the country we fled,
looking for our house,
searching for my other,

circle round and round,
unbelieving. What wind blew it?

What wind blew us, blows us,
north, south?

What moon pulls me two ways?

I balance myself on the edge,
face el otro lado, my twin,
my double, my near

and distant other.

Gold Nuggets

Brother-in-law Rube and his jazz ensemble
play a smooth *Bésame mucho,* slow dancing
followed by kicking and spinning to *Hava Nagila,*
best man, maitre'd Majarian, pops, glides,
and pours his gift, two cases of French champagne,
sisters toss salads, carve turkeys they roasted at midnight,
housekeeper friends from Nayarit steam
and serve homemade tamales, rice, and beans,
arrange bouquets of white gladioli,
uncles tend Tecates in ice buckets
as guests arrive by bus, train, truck, taxi, limo, jalopy, and jet
from Tokyo, Mazatlán, Ensenada, East L.A., Riverside, Watts,
papá and his sister drive up in a jeep from Ensenada, papá
handsome, charming, and awkward as always in a suit,
tía comfortable in a mink stole even in October heatwave,
mamá sitting next to them wearing her beauty like a big diamond,
in black chiffon dress and black, veiled hat,
color she wears only to funerals and weddings,
classmate Hideo capturing moods with pro Minolta,
uncles and skinny boy cousins pin green bills
on white veil for the honor of twirling bride
around Inglewood's Knights of Columbus Hall,
Cheers! from friends, teachers, and classmates
not long ago juggling jobs in Shanghai, Palestine, Jamaica, Panama,
now trying to survive in Hollywood, Silverlake, Hawthorne, Gardena,
Cubano baker neighbor cuts thick slices of rum cream cake,

middle-aged couple from Beverly Hills--
who take in Japanese houseboys--sit stunned,
asking in whispers what two college students can manage
such a dazzling feast,
mamá, who can hear whispers and thoughts, says,
Cada pobrete lo que tiene mete,
loosely, Each poor devil puts in his two cents,
or gold nuggets.
¡Salud! Kanpai! ¡Chinchín!

"The Hands"

Las manos

Según la luz, del sol greñudo
o de la luna, de la sombra
de un tamarindo al mediodía
o de una capilla al atardecer,
las manos, mis manos, tus manos,
se verán color de crema o de canela,
rosadas, rojas, negras o amarillas--
nuestra herencia.

Estas son manos de congas,
de requintos, güiros, claves, bongós
y timbales, de maracas, charangos,
guitarrones y marimbas,
castañuelas, panderetas y címbalos
--tin tin timbaleo tingo--
estas manos cantan, bailan, palmean
al son del maíz rumbeando
rumbo a ser tortilla,
estas manos redondean albóndigas
y sueños, circundan cinturas y suspiros,
pelan plátanos, máscaras y mangos,
suman, multiplican en pizarras
y en comales, estas manos
hablan español con soltura,
calientan, quitan calentura,
a veces escriben poesía,
a veces la recitan, estas manos
pudieran quitar todas las penas.

Estas manos, atadas con siglos de cuerdas
a hornos, mesas, escobas, trapeadores,
a bandejas y plumeros, a martillos,
serruchos, picos, palas y asadones,
restriegan pisos, platos y mentiras,
recogen fresas, uvas, insultos y cebollas,
siembran maíz, yerbabuena, cilantro
y esperanza, poco a poco desentierran
nuestra historia.

Estas manos, tan inmensas, tan pequeñas,
dos chuparrosas, atadas, quietas,
se desatan, gritan, se cierran en un puño
de amargura, de coraje, de impaciencia,
estas manos alzadas se abren,
exigen lo mismo que producen,
que están dando, estas manos
sonríen en su triunfo.

The Hands

Depending on the light, of the tangled sun
or of the moon, of the shade
of a tamarind at noon or a chapel at dusk,
the hands, these hands, my hands,
your hands, will appear cream or cinnamon,
pink, red, black or yellow--our heritage.

These are hands of congas, of requintos,
güiros, claves, bongos, and timbales,
of maracas, charangos, guitarrones,
and marimbas, castanets, tambourines,
and cymbals--tin tin timbaleo tingo--
these hands sing, dance, clap
to the beat of corn rumbeando
on its way to becoming a tortilla,
these hands round albondigas
and dreams, circle waists and sighs,
peel bananas, masks, and mangos,
add, subtract on blackboards and griddles,
these hands speak fluent Spanish,
they warm, they reduce fevers,
sometimes they write poetry,
sometimes they recite it, these hands
could take away all pain.

These hands, tied by centuries of rope
to ovens, tables, brooms, mops, trays and dusters,
to hammers, saws, picks, hoes, and shovels,

scrub floors, plates, and lies,
pick strawberries, grapes, insults, and onions,
plant corn, mint, hope, and cilantro,
piece by piece they unearth
our history.

These hands, so large, so small,
two hummingbirds, quiet, still,
unbind, shout, close into a fist
of sorrow, of anger, of impatience,
these raised hands open,
demand the same as they produce,
as they are giving, these hands
smile in triumph.

2.

La frontera

es un muro de mentiras con púas,
una cadena de suspiros,
un corazón palpitante,
una vieja herida.

Aladino vende lámparas
maravillosas. Alí Baba junta
a sus ladrones, el LLanero Solitario
se une a los Texas Rangers,
Darth Vader entrena a los Storm Troopers,
El Santo lucha contra Batman,
La LLorona aúlla.

Chaplin y Cantinflas suben un cerro
bamboleándose, bajan rodando,
Siqueiros pinta el cielo
color sangre, Dalí pega
una luna morada, enciende
la sonrisa del gato Cheshire.

Las escondidas, patear el bote,
indios y vaqueros,
ajedrez, dominó, tin Marín,
la lotería, cada uno
con un mundo a cuestas.

Veredas de vidrios rotos
luminosos como estrellas.

Una puerta atrancada sin paredes,
una ventana rota
donde un zopilote se sienta
a esperar.

Una cruz de piedras
extendida a los cuatro puntos
cardinales, cada piedra una plegaria,
cada plegaria una piedra que murmura.

Un río seco, los peces boqueando
en aire, aire de lunas giratorias,
cama de piedra, sueños de palomas
fosforescentes en vuelo.

Caballos voladores, balas perdidas,
piedras por el aire, ojos ultravioleta
que olfatean calor, atrapan suspiros.

La frontera es un muro de mentiras
con púas, un suspiro de cadenas,
un corazón palpitante,
es una herida nueva
en una cortada vieja.

The Border

is a wall of barbed lies,
a chain of sighs,
a heart pounding,
an old wound.

Aladdin hawks his magic
lamps, Ali Baba rounds up
his thieves, Lone Ranger
rejoins Texas Rangers,
El Santo wrestles Batman,
La Llorona howls.

Chaplin and Cantinflas
waddle up a hill, roll down,
Siqueiros paints the sky blood red,
Dalí pastes a purple moon, lights
the smile of the Cheshire cat.

Hide and seek, kick-the-can,
Cowboys and Indians,
chess, dominoes, la lotería,
a world loaded on each back.

Trails of broken glass
glittering like stars.

A bolted door without walls,
a broken window where
a vulture sits and waits.

A cross of stones,
each stone a prayer,
each prayer a murmuring stone.

A dry river, fish gasping in air,
air of whirling moons,
bed of rocks, dreams of
phosphorescent doves in flight.

Flying horses, flying bullets,
flying rocks, ultra-violet eyes
sensing heat, capturing sighs.

The border is a wall of barbed lies,
a sigh of chains,
a pounding heart,
a fresh wound on an old cut.

"English con Salsa"

English con Salsa

Welcome to ESL 100, English Surely Latinized,
inglés con chile y cilantro, English as American
as Benito Juárez. Welcome, muchachos from Xochicalco
learn the language of dólares and dolores, of kings
and queens, of Donald Duck and Batman. Holy Toluca!
In four months you'll be speaking like George Washington,
in four weeks you can ask, More coffee? in two months
you can say, May I take your order? In one year you
can ask for a raise, cool as the Tuxpan River.

Welcome, muchachas from Teocaltiche, in this class
we speak English refrito, English con sal y limón,
English thick as mango juice, English poured from
a clay jug, English tuned like a requinto from Uruapan,
English lighted by Oaxacan dawns, English spiked
with mezcal from Mitla, English with a red cactus
flower blooming in its heart.

Welcome, welcome, amigos del sur, bring your Zapotec
tongues, your Nahuatl tones, your patience of pyramids,
your red suns and golden moons, your guardian angels,
your duendes, your patron saints, Santa Tristeza,
Santa Alegría, San Todolopuede. We will sprinkle
holy water on pronouns, make the sign of the cross
on past participles, jump like fish from Lake Pátzcuaro
on gerunds, pour tequila from Jalisco on future perfects,
says shoes and shit, grab a cool verb and a pollo loco
and dance on the walls like chapulines.

When a teacher from La Jolla, or a cowboy from Santee
asks you, Do you speak English? You'll answer, Sí,
yes, simón, of course, I love English!

And you'll hum
a Mixtec chant that touches la tierra and the heavens.

English con salsa

Bienvenidos al ESL 100, *English Surely Latinized,*
inglés con chile y cilantro, *English* tan *American*
como Benito Juárez. Bienvenidos muchachos de Xochicalco,
aprendan el idioma de dólares y dolores, de reyes
y reinas, del Pato Donald y Batman. *Holy Toluca!*
En cuatro meses estarán hablando como George Washington.
En cuatro semanas podran preguntar: *More coffee?* En dos
meses podran decir: *May I take your order?* En un año
podran pedir un aumento, con la frescura del RíoTuxpan.

Bienvenidas, muchachas de Teocaltiche, en esta clase
hablamos *English* refrito, *English* con sal y limón.
English espeso como jugo de mango, *English vaciado*
de un jarrito de barro, *English* bien afinado como requinto de Uruapan,
English alumbrado por madrugadas oaxaqueñas, *English*
con piquete de mezcal de Mitla, *English* con flor de cactus
roja abierta en el centro de su corazón.

Welcome, welcome, amigos del sur, traigan sus lenguas
zapotecas, sus tonos náhuatl, su paciencia de pirámides,
sus soles rojos y sus lunas doradas, sus ángeles de la guarda,
sus duendes, sus santos patrones, Santa Tristeza, Santa Alegría,
San Todolopuede. Rociaremos agua bendita
sobre los pronombres, le haremos la señal de la cruz
a los participios pasivos, brincaremos como peces
del Lago de Pátzcuaro en los gerundios, vaciaremos
tequila de Jalisco sobre los futuros perfectos, diremos
shoes y *shit,* tomaremos un verbo bien *cool* y un pollo loco
y bailaremos en las paredes como chapulines,

Cuando una maestra de La Jolla o un vaquero de Santee les pregunte: *Do you speak English?* Contestarán: Sí, *yes*, simón, *of course. I love English!*

Y murmurarás
un canto mixteco que conmoverá a la tierra y al cielo.

Border Tango

A sultry night in San Diego,
students of English, newly arrived
from el otro lado, discuss
perils of la frontera, ask
the red-haired burly Argentino
what problems he faced
crossing.

Sebastián, shrugging his big shoulders,
says in lilting Spanish,
¿Qué problemas? Me aplaudieron.

As he tells it,
he jumped the fence,
bowed,

trekked through hills
under a full moon beam.

These, his pampas,
and he, steel-tongued,
rhyme-dueling, roaming gaucho.

Maybe there's a gaucho in many
a crosser, a fated moment
of tragic glory.

Like that night
when Sebastián arrived in San Diego
to a welcoming committee
of one--

into the arms of a woman in red
who tangoed the span of the Coronado Bridge.

El tango de la frontera

Una noche bochornosa en San Diego,
estudiantes de inglés, recien llegados
del otro lado, lamentaban
los peligros de la frontera, preguntaron
al pelirrojo y fornido argentino
si había enfrentado problemas
al cruzar.

Sebastián encogió sus grandes hombros
y dijo en melodioso español,
¿Qué problemas? Me aplaudieron.

Según él,
saltó la cerca,
hizo reverencia

y caminó por los cerros
bajo un rayo de luna llena.

Estas, sus pampas
y él, un gaucho errante,
lengua de acero,
duelista de rimas.

Tal vez hay un gaucho en muchos
que cruzan, un predestinado momento
de gloria trágica.

Como esa noche,
cuando Sebastián llegó a San Diego
a un comité de bienvenida
de uno--

a los brazos de una mujer de rojo
que tangeó el espacio del Puente Coronado.

Under a Blooming Sun

In North San Diego   kingdom
of flowers   village men
from Southern Mexico
and Guatemala   bend over
low-lying rainbows
of poppy   tulip
under a blooming sun
pressing them close to
dizzying rose   lavender
brown hands tender-gathering
blossoms for dollars they send
to women left grinding corn
holy maize   (engineers
in U.S. labs convert unholy)
they carry sacks of tortillas
to sell at their village mercado
one   a village of women   all
the men working in California
women who wear huipiles
they embroider with unfading
roses   zinnias

Sudden Journeys

Midnight   I dial the night
for your voice not cracked
by fists   gun   nightstick

your voice not silenced
by men with badges   without

who freeze your breath
at bus stops after
your twelve-hour workday

The night is silent   the journey
unplanned   destination
unknown

van   ward   cell   nightmare
where you crouch

desert where you trudge
condition a guess   a fear
wounded   way worn   lost

One moon rules the night
moon that lights your path
moon that drags you to edged terrain

in a cycle of sudden journeys

Azafrán

I see them on my way to work: a gathering of men huddling
by the straw-dry San Diego River, men from Acatlán,
Tamazula, Tepehuanes, who claim the unpaved sidewalk
on Riverside Drive in Lakeside, their office,

> the 7-Eleven across the street, their diner
> serving up bitter coffee and a sugary bite--
> the day's meal--unless a cowboy in an SUV stops
> to offer a day's work and the lucky one is hauled
> away with all he's got: hard muscles, skilled hands,
> and a furious will to survive.

The day after 9/11, a stream of SUVS, trucks, and jalopies rolls down
Riverside flapping stars and stripes, one to five a car.

> Driving back home--flagless--I catch sight of
> the men from different towns in Mexico--
> all-American boys now--

chasing away an Arab man to the other side of the river,
shouting, *Bad man, bad man, go, go!* sparks of fear
shooting out of dark eyes.

> Undulant flags dwindle to one--
> confederate flag still flies above nearby house--
> and a gathering of jornaleros from other towns in Mexico
> now claims Riverside, hustling a day's work,
> dreaming of turn of fortunes: full time work
> for a small plot back in their villages.

On the other side of the river surges El Cajon, where
I run errands. My first stop: a nameless market for
warm tortillas, the high stack gone by noon, the owner
brothers on their way to a village in Guanajuato.

> The new owner is a burly Shiite who sings praises
> to Sistani, who one day beams when I recite Hafez
> and another day angrily recounts an Al-Jazeera report
> of a brutal attack at a hospital in Iraq. *They're Spanish!*
> *Spanish!* (meaning Hispanic) he fumes as we clutch
> our tortillas.

The following week, the Shiite announces he's returning to
Iraq to see his other wife. Two Mexican men paying for tortillas
and pan dulce lean toward him, *Why you have two wives?*
Why? Why? He rakes in our dollars for his ticket home.

> Now a Kurd is selling tortillas, urging me,
> *Come to Iraq, to the north, safe and beautiful*
> *as San Diego.*

A Chaldean takes over, tells me Saddam called the Chaldeans
the flowers of Iraq. Moving closer, he says, *Mexicans are*
the flowers of America.

> I drag my old Nissan to my favorite carwash, find it
> Iraqi-owned, men from Michoacán and Zacatecas
> replaced by Kurds, five surrounding me,
> polishing my car with silent concentration.

The new immigrants: at last count, fifteen-thousand strong
in the country's second largest Little Iraq.

Cruising down Main Street, I see a gathering of men
with intense eyes in animated conversation
in front of Hajji Baba restaurant.

Women with long dresses and beige or black headscarves
walk toward a market where, at the entrance, statues of
a camel and St. Jude welcome them.

Looking for good saffron, I follow them in
and the lively chatting subsides.

The Chaldean owner pulls out a small tin can from a glass case
on the counter, places it in my palm like a gold coin, tells me,
Very good kind. From Spain.

I hold the fiery herb that'll turn my cheeks
to pomegranates, this precious spice--azafrán--
that conjures up hanging gardens, trilling fountains,
almond blossoms, gazelle eyes, musulmanes,
judios, y cristianos--the flowering of al-Andalus.

The Iraqi merchant looks intently at the saffron and at me, says,
Spanish. Very good kind.

3.

Spells

You charm me with a smile of let me
show you the treasures of Oaxaca.

I follow you to Santo Domingo, am dazzled by
gold dome ceiling sculpted
by Mixtecos--not for Crown or Church--
to worship the sun.

Prayers for safe journeys north and vows
to return spiral towards shimmering dome.

Under a moonlit flamboyán, you sing
tender isthmus songs casting a red spell on the night
and nights to come.

                              Once again
you glide to my house like a forest cloud
with your broad chest that holds mountain air
and a heart in blossom. You touch me
with potter's hands that fondle clay into song.

I taste you in the heat of mezcal,
in the sweetness of orange slices.

Yes, I whisper, and dare to try
a morsel of grasshopper taco, falling
under the spell of return:

to the chiming of ancient dialects,
La Zandunga sung in Zapotec, to el Zócalo
with its hanging moon, danzones on marimba,
and baskets of gardenias.

I'll be pulled by a mouth electric as the breeze
from the Papaloapan River,
the flutter of bodies and hearts
opening like flor de calabaza.

"Spells"

Dark Nectar

Sundays, women roast cacao
seeds at mercado Tlacolula:
women who long for their men,
working in California.

They grind the seeds to powder
on volcanic stone, as they've done
for centuries, the dark aroma
filling the clear Oaxacan sky.

We ride home on a rickety bus
singing boleros all the way.
Then brew chocolate de agua,
the pleasure of kings and peasants,
with honey and vanilla,
that black orchid.

Under the Zapotec moon
your body glows, a shade between
honey and cocoa. In your mouth
I savor the bittersweet
nectar, hold the spell
on my tongue.

Under the Eagle Sun

1

In Northern Mexico
tías yelled warnings
to play in the shade
as we ran out of the house
to skip, prance, and spin all day
under the eagle sun.

2

In Southern Mexico
dark men call out, *güera*,
as if saying, *querida*.

The eagle sun plants kisses,
darkens our faces.

Under a gold moon
tugging at the blood,
he whispers, *morenita*,
she sighs, *prieto*,
mi amor.

The Fruit That Bites
Oaxaca City

I tumble on a mercado
in an overlit back street,
boleros steam the air,
spices fire salsas and spells,
cacao smoke strokes the skin,
cut fruit dresses in red,
a ripening sun chases me
to shaded side.

Sun or shade,
my skin and eyes heat up
with every step,
hot liquid gushes
out of my orbs,
nose and throat pulse,
feel stung by cactus needles.

Through watery eyes I behold
two women with color of fire huipiles,
reigning--centuries--over
orange red purple black pyramids
of dried chile--ancho pasilla árbol
habanero mulato guajillo manzano
chipotle--powder-grinding it,
searing air, chatting, laughing.

My feet quicken, my body thirsts
for a Pacífico, one glass
to stumble laughing and crying
in capsicum attack.

My body is shapeshifting--
California roadrunner heads home,
demands water--gulps splashes rinses--
flops down on bed, coaxes breeze
and fan to help quell fire.

I drift back to five,
sitting by mamá at the kitchen table,
a pickled jalapeño jar--Holy Capsicum Annuum--
gleaming before her. One green flame
flies onto her plate, into her mouth,
half disappears, lights up her face.
Papá and daughters, who never eat chile,
watch tittering.

I dare to sneak a tiny bite,
fruit from Jalapa bites back.
Red-tongued, red-faced, red-eyed demon
springs up, swigs water,
returns to table, peers at mamá
finishing off bitten biting pepper--
glowing, laughing mamá
who outlived everybody.

"Ode to the Tortilla"

Ode to the Tortilla

Daily I say, pass me a tortilla,
as if saying, pass me the sun,
the moon, kiss me.

Round blessing, our daily tlayuda,
our sacred tlaxcalli.

Spoon of seamstresses, meat of bricklayers,
inspiration of carpenters, bread of the unemployed.

¡Santa Tortilla de cada día!
You bless with your smoky scent
those who love you.

Child of the golden seed stolen back from hell
by Quetzalcóatl
so we can persist on earth,
taste heaven.

Hard little seed of generosity,
you bathe in limestone, soak, swell,
shed your hardness for us.
You roll with metate and metlapil,
those volcanoes.

Chanting hands shape your full moon face,
the comal kisses you hotly on both cheeks,
prepares you for my mouthful of kisses.

Daily I say, pass me a tortilla,
edible sun, nutritious moon,
planetary delight,
I want to celebrate my body of corn,
the gold light of my spirit.

Loyalty to the Humble

In the streets of Guatemala, undercover agents
lingered at the stands of las tortilleras,
campesinas Mayas who set up shop at dawn
to offer the city its daily sustenance.
They asked which houses had bought more
than a dozen tortillas. That's how the houses
where guerrillas hid were discovered,
los guerrilleros betrayed by their loyalty
to the humble tortilla.

Lealtad al humilde

En las calles de Guatemala, agentes secretos
se detenían en los puestos de las tortilleras,
campesinas mayas que abrían sus negocios
al amanecer, ofreciendo al pueblo el sustento diario.
Preguntaban cuáles casas habían comprado más
de una docena de tortillas. Y es así como las casas
donde se escondían los guerrilleros eran descubiertas,
los guerrilleros traicionados por su lealtad
a la humilde tortilla.

In the Land of Zapata

Ten thousand maestros seize
the heart of Oaxaca,
arrive from la Selva Lacandona
with the mantle and stride of Zapata,
el Río Papaloapan's electric charge,
Puerto Escondido's ten foot waves,
la Sierra Juárez's cedar smoke and squalls,
la Sierra Mixe's 500-year-resistance.

It's difficult to walk on this path
throbbing with drums and complaints,
chants and testimonies,
guitars and demands: Classrooms. Books.
Wages for a stack of tortillas
and a jugful of dignity
to grace the daily table.

The grass of el Zócalo flattens and dries
with so many bodies and grievances,
la marimba plays in other skies,
los turistas flee to Cancún.

Students roam the streets, some lamenting
lost lessons, others offer agua y fruta,
a cluster of thank yous to los maestros
who trekked through suns and moons
to raise one quetzal-feathered voice

so they--los maestros y sus estudiantes--
won't be forced to risk becoming

       white crosses

              on the passage north.

Comparsas

These nights nobody is serious
or seriously dead

With or without a body
these are nights of sleepless
candles   Velas desveladas

La Calaca prods the crowd
to dance toward graves
swig mezcal to let loose
soulcries

Marigold   Cockscomb
Pan de muertos Sugar skull
Calavera dulcecita

Drums   Horns   Cymbals
at full blast tease La Calaca

She rolls her shoulders
rattles her hips   snaps her teeth
taunts--

Baila   Baila tu rumba
My feet are nimble   winged

> Days of the Dead
> Oaxaca City

Woman Run Over by Little Devil
on Christmas Eve

She wept with pain,
then sighed with relief
because the little devil--
a dolly loaded with trash--
hadn't broken her bones.

She cried with rage
at the conductor of el diablito
for not paying attention
but felt grateful he wasn't
maneuvering a bus.

She moaned loudly
when a neighbor chided her
for not noticing the little devil
but thanked him for reminding her
that what matters
is not jumping out of bed
but landing on your feet,
holding steady
on the reeling earth,
sidestepping speeding devils
and flying trash.

Butterfly Woman

My laughter is a black night
full of green birds

My sighs are a flock of crows
diving in a smoky sky
from the heights of pines

I am a woman who writes
under the spell of two tongues
to a whispering flute
and the music of light rain

A woman who seeks
A woman who finds

A butterfly woman
history of migration
in my multipatterned wings

4.

Origins

When papá tells me
Mexicanos have origins in Tibet,
his smile an exclamation,

it's hard to argue with him,
gazing at his tan skin stretched taut
over Himalayan cheekbones.

Ice-age girl from Yucatán
rises from a cave lake
to tell a similar tale.

Papá's laughter vibrates the room,
resonates in the singing bowl
of my body.

His usual way
of beginning and ending
an argument.

Santa Anas blow chili powder
breath on prayer flags in my garden,
ignite sutras.

Sky sisters,
Guadalupe and Tara,
cast a green glow on my altar.

We have origins in Tibet,
papá's smile insists.

Maybe, I say,
as I look into the mirror
of his face.

Our resemblance provokes me
to a burst of laughter: ice crystals
melting.

Infinite Wheel of Desire

The yoga instructor never looked passionately into her eyes, embraced her with urgency, or kissed her with ardor. He sat in front of her in a lotus position and said in a voice that rose from his diaphragm, *I want to realize myself with you.*

The music professor wanted to tune her ear. He turned off all the lights in the room, to improve the acoustics, and played a tape of fertility music from Indonesia with which the gods multiply.

I want to make love with you. Tonight. Now, said the Ramakrishnananda disciple. *If tomorrow I pass away, I will leave unfinished business, and be born again and again in a never-ending wheel of desire.*

El círculo infinito del deseo

El maestro de yoga nunca la miró apasionadamente a los ojos,
ni la abrazó con urgencia, ni la besó con ardor. Se sentó frente
a ella en postura de loto y le dijo con una voz que le brotaba del
diagframa, *Quiero realizarme contigo.*

El profesor de música deseaba afinar su oído. Apagó todas las
luces en el cuarto, para mejorar la acústica, y tocó una cinta de
música de Indonesia, para la fertilidad, multiplicante de dioses.

Quiero hacer el amor contigo. Esta noche. Ahora, dijo el discípulo
de Ramakrishnananda. Si me muero mañana dejaré un asunto
pendiente y seguiré naciendo vida tras vida en un círculo sin fin
de deseo.

Religion Knocks at My Door

Religion spies my Spanish surname
on my mailbox, flies up stairs
in gray suit and tie,

Religion knocks at my door,
confesses he was lost
but found himself. Praise Jesus!

¡Ay Jesús! I like your sweet cane
accent, you must come from Veracruz.
He smiles. Frowns.
This conversation doesn't fit
in his briefcase.

Revelations: Decadence.
Repentence. Sobriety.

Behind tight jaw vibrate
drunk-on-love-cloud-splitting gritos.
Stiff pants can't hide hips
born to undulate under mango trees.

Religion sways at my door,
awakens religious fervor
to save him.

Little Miracles

For decades I braved
the speed-spooked freeways
and streets of Southern California,
steering Chevys and Nissans past
allotted life spans.

When the overworked vehicle
huffed and stalled on a highway,
side street, or back road,
most often than not help arrived
in a smooth-running carcacha
with a crew of muchachos
from Mexican villages
who sprang out of their coche
to ease-open my hood, tinker
and coax until the motor
shuddered awake.

Accepting only a gracias
for the little miracle,
they waved goodbye
and faded away,

the revived jalopy and I,
once again daring the road.

The Pepper Tree

Survivor of gusts
of wind, fire, smoke,
lightning, hailstorms,
drought.

Deep-rooted, thick-skinned,
bushy-haired Brazilian pepper--
my aging family's shield
from East San Diego sun's
daily arrows--

convalesces in patio,
cracked and bare, limbs torn
and flung to the ground by wrath
of an all-night Santa Ana.

Victor the gardener who says
he's from Oaxacalifornia,
prunes pepper, smiles
at moist bark, predicts
shade by summer.

On waking, I look out
at a new vista: stark
tree with exposed gold bark,

newly visible hills
of neighing, bronco-riding,
gas-guzzling, flag-waving,
KSON country town

with habit of glowering
flame red, cycling
grief black, born-again green.

January: hot
windstorms, cold squalls.
The Pacific pounding our houses.

Years-long drought followed by
month-long deluge,
slick mud.

My family with roots
in this and other soils
begins to dislodge,
our tendrils loosening
their grip.

With budding green tongues
the pepper announces spring

while I soak in my living room
flooded with gold light.

Árbol sagrado

Fruta sensual

Regalo
de los dioses

Canto tus nombres
ahuaca
aguaco
aguacate
ahuacatl

Gift
of the gods

Staple
of Mexico
for millennia

Born in Tehuacán Valley
in Coxcatlán Cave

Fragrant family
Lauraceae
laurel y canela

Oro verde
michoacano

Se cantan tus nombres
con requinto de Uruapan

Green gold
number one
food export

seized bruised
by steel hands
of narcos
the exporters'
extorters

high cost
in country
of origin

Migrants
welcomed north
south east west
welcomed with open
mouths in every land

Our love for you
obsessive deforests
jungles woodlands

Mother fruit
nurtures by nature
fruit with no sugar
fats balanced
mother lode
of minerals vitamins
nutrient rich and
satisfying

Avocado
Persea americana
State fruit of California
gift from Atlexco, Puebla
flourishes in San Diego
in Fallbrook The Friendly Village
once home to Tom Metzger
Grand Dragon of Klan founder of
WAR White Aryan Resistance
no doubt watched Super Bowl
with Corona six-pack
tubs of corn chips
and guacamole

Aguacatitos
startle customers 2017
Whole Foods sells to Amazon
lower prices promise
display sign shouts
LARGE AVOCADOS $1.00
avos the size of chicken eggs
I exit WF along with
a slew of employees

Mexican avocados
near my San Diego home
in thriving market
$3.00 buys you one avo
not from nearby farm
larger carbon footprint

Avocado groves
60,000 acres in California

breathe in carbon dioxide
exhale oxygen

In my garden
all seeds sprout manifold
shades of geen red
yellow purple orange
plot once avocado grove

California roll
vinegared rice nori seaweed
crab creamy avocado invented
in 60s L.A. Little Tokyo
sushi chef Ichiro Mashita
Kanpai Ichiro!
Kanpai Fusion!

Ahuacatl
testículos de árbol
fruit of fertility
grows in pairs
parejas

Eres el aguacate
de mi torta

Los Mexicas
master cultivators
belligerent cruel
wielded more than
obsidian knives

conceived canals
public housing

functional and beautiful
steam baths daily
chinampas urban farming
brightened days with
cochineal red

farmed organic
meals plant-based
elotl papatl tomatl
frijoles y calabaza
cultivated concoted
aphrodisiacs chilli
xocolatl tlilzuchitl
black orchid vanilla
vegan butter ahuacatl
foods that nourish
pleasure the world's
palates

Ahuacamolli
salsa de aguacate
guacamole recipe a gift
from el dios tolteca Quetzalcóatl
ahuacatl chilli tomatl
cebolla cilantro
squeeze of lime
pinch of salt
for the soul

Quetzalcóatl
Mexicas
ahuacatl
árbol del amor

fruta sensual
y sagrada

thank you
gracias
tlazocamati

"Árbol sagrado"

Omens

A lizard drags its tail
through a crack
in the world

to lie on my altar
under a skylight
among saints and Buddhas.

For days the gecko sits still
and silent: a green monk
revealing the way to lizardy heaven,

while on the oaks, crows cry out--
for us to decode--
the names of the dying.

La Calaca is stalking us, warns mamá.

The phone channels another hard sell
from a mortuary.
I'm not interested, I groan.
She persists, insists I prepare.

My relatives, blessed
or cursed with long lives,
parade before me--
papá's luminous body
walking backwards.

I bow to my kin, to papá,
to the gold-green herald
sun-worshipping on my altar--

    master of stillness,
    of vanishing--

suddenly chasing after its tail,
transforming to spinning wheel
    to whirling zero.

Walking Away

1

The last time I saw papá walk,
he was walking away
from me, crossing the border
to his home in el sur.

I stayed in el norte,
watching him leave, again
and again saying goodbye,
our lives defined by this
split,

defined by contacts and fractures
like this seismic earth he studied.

2

When I learned to walk
out of our house, I ventured often
into his woodshop, attracted by
scent of cedar, maple, and pine,
sawdust sprinkled on black hair,
a red flannel shirt I stroked
for warmth, a tuned-guitar smile
that would soon brighten
another house.

3

Years of brief encounters later,
in el sur, in a house of sons,
in a room of cedar, lies
a man who can't recall
the name of the daughter
named after him.

¿Quién soy, Papá? ¿Cómo me llamo?

He's thirty again, volume and romance
in his voice. *I know who you are.*
Mona Lisa...

Laughter, his lifelong antidote for pain,
has left his body. The tuned smile,
melodious voice, and scent of cedar
cling to the end.

The ogre that gnaws his bones
drugged numb, he gazes at me
and says with lucidity that burns
like barbed wire, *So near*
and so far.

Equating Zero

The night math wizard papá crossed
toward the radiance of stars,
I was not at his bedside.

A messenger arrived at my house
to announce his passing: A loud cricket
sat on my altar and sang three nights.

Three nights I dreamed of footloose
papá with his electric body,
superluminous smile, papá still
equating zero: the infinity of love.

Between Worlds

My sister decided to leave
hospice for home.

On her nightstand glared neon-colored pills
sorted in an ice-cube tray. Each pill
was a blessing, a curse.

Daily for one week she asked,
What am I?

Each day in a mirror a woman warrior appeared,
dimmed.

In her dreams she saw a bird
in flames swirling to smoke, ashes.

I'm between worlds, she whispered,

offered agua fresca and mangos
to las abuelas who arrived
dressed in brilliant indigo light.

My sister stepped out of her house
of fire and ice, tissue and dreams,
terror and bone

and followed las abuelas' blue trail
to another star.

Rainbowoman

She lived out loud, in elemental colors.
Can see her: red hair, purple velvet coat,
mamá at Midnight Mass, rivaling
the moonlit stained-glass windows.

Can see her: regal and feline
from her gold eyes to her silk-stockinged
feet, a teen girl sliding out of a limo
at a Hollywood studio where her long-fingered
hands nimbly sewed costumes into perfect fits.

Back in the limo with skin aglow
from a job well done and a secret dream:
admiring her own designs on screen
in the days of Garbo and Dolores del Río.

Always on stage with her comedic wit--
Stop talking while I'm interrupting--
She lived her truth: *Women should be seen
and heard.*

She ignored bad press, defined herself:
Smart. Witty. Shrewd.

And never past her prime. At 80, hearing--
You must have been beautiful when you were young--
quipped--*And what's wrong with me now.*

Mamá lived almost a century
following one piece of advice: her own.

On her last breath--a winter day of
window-rattling torrential rain--a rainbow
streaked across the gray California sky.

The Blue Crow

A hot spring day still with fear
of conflagrations and vipers,
a pale yellow/black striped six-footer
halted my afternoon walk.

Faster than I could decide,
freeze or flee, a blue jay dived
from the heights of a pine,
pecked the snake's head and hovered
above it watching it turn
and slither away.

No caw, hiss, rustle, or shriek.
Not a sound. Only the heart
of all things throbbing.

El cuervo azul

Un día de primavera inmovilizado
por el temor a conflagraciones
y viboras, una amarilla clara/
rayas negras, de seis pies detuvo
mi paseo de la tarde.

Mas rápido que la decisión
de estarme quieta o huír,
un arrendajo azul bajó en picado
desde la cima de un pino,
picoteó a la vibora en la cabeza
y se cernió sobre ella, mirándola
deslizarse y retroceder.

Ni un graznido, siseo, crujir o alarido.
Todo quedo. Sólo el corazón
de las cosas palpitando.

Those Birds

Those birds that sing before dawn,
do they love the darkness
or are they sensing imminent light?

Li Po

How do you know I don't know
what gives pleasure to fish.

—Chuang Tzu to a logician

The day Venus became a beauty mark on the Sun's face,
I celebrated my birthday with a Siamese fish leaping
into my stream for double good luck.

I named him Li Po because he shined acrobatic:
a drunk poet longing to stroke the moon.

All day he darted around (his two-quart lagoon).
Says Chuang Tzu...*such is the pleasure of fish.*

I held fish treats--dried blood beads--above his pool
to feel his bitekiss.

When I sang, Hello Li Po! to the well of his heart,
it startled him out of his pond, wingfins a violet shimmer.

A dozen waning moons turned Li Po recluse.
From behind a stone Buddha he emerged a floating boat.

For one moon, when I glanced at his empty abode,
there was heart-leaping Li Po suspended above it--
stillness his pleasure now--waiting
for my song of hellos.

Slowing

I speeded in California fearing being rear-bumped
off highways. Flying down I-5 one day, I slowed down,
forever, recalling a mortuary billboard, SLOW DOWN.
WE CAN WAIT.

I stroll on cracked sidewalks with small steps
of a kimono-clad, geta-wearing lady
on plum-scented and cherry-lined streets
of Portland,

step aside for the coffee-revved cane-carrying
speeding by that leave me asking,
Where are you going so fast?

I need a flock of sparrows to help me sing
praises to slow love   mouths   hands
bodies slow blooming in   long   nights

My slow motion life smooth lands in the center
of a round black cushion, still body
startled by LA-rush hour reckless mind,
thought after thought a necklace of crushed roses
and skulls.

Slowly I learn to sit at sunrise at sunset
thoughts arising vanishing body mind
relaxing in the pause.

Walking on Earth

On my walk on earth
may I greet everyone
with a silent blessing

walk steady on shaky land
soft footsteps on rocky soil
cruising crows soundless above me

on dark nights
walk with green birds
luminous jasmine

on full moons
walk with the flute player
a satchel of songs

walk on earth's edge
sky's rim
where worlds meet

On my walk on earth
may I greet all that lives
with a silent blessing

bless what must end

Notes

English con salsa was translated into Spanish by Mexican poet and translator Claire Joysmith.

"The Double" is for Olivia Ruiz Marrujo.

"Las manos" and "The Hands" were first published in my chapbook *Comiendo lumbe/Eating Fire.*

"In the Land of Zapata" is for Rosaura Sánchez.

"Butterfly Woman" was inspired by the chants of María Sabina of Oaxaca.

"The Pepper Tree" is for my sister Carmen Figueroa.

"Walking on Earth" was inspired by Nahuatl and Navajo chants and by Zen Master Thich Nhat Hanh.

Acknowledgments to writers who helped me

Mil gracias to the writer-scholars who, throughout the years, have offered me inspiration, insight, teaching, and overall support: Olivia Ruiz Marrujo, Rosaura Sánchez, Beatrice Pita, Claire Joysmith, Sandra Cisneros, Alurista, in memoriam to Joan Lindgren and Steve Kowit, and to my sister Carmen Figueroa. Y mil gracias for the recognition of my work to the writer-editors, Edward Vidaurre, Odilia Galván Rodriguez, and Emmy Pérez, and to Avery Castillo and Priscilla Celina Suarez for their caring help in the production of my book. To all of you, my deepest gratitude.

Acknowledgments

A heartfelt thank you to the editors of the following publications:

Adanna: "The Gift"

BoomerLit: "Walking Away"

California Quarterly Review: "Woman Run Over by Little Devil on Christmas Eve," "Religion Knocks at My Door"

Calyx: "Gold Nuggets"

City Works: "The Fruit that Bites"

Earth's Daughters: "Li Po"

Fearless Poetry Series: Touching: Poems of Love, Longing, and Desire: "Dark Nectar"

Huizache: "Loyalty to the Humble," "In the Land of Zapata," "Sudden Journeys," "Under the Blooming Sun," "Árbol sagrado"

Mizna: "Azafran"

Native West Press: Staying Wildly Sane in a Mad World: "The Blue Crow"

Off the Coast: "Border Tango"

Pedestal: "Omens"

Pilgrimage: "Acts of Protest"

Pocket Books: "Under the Pomegranate Tree," "Infinite Wheel of Desire"

Quills Edge: 50/50: Poems and Translations by Women over Fifty: "Under the Eagle Sun," "Walking on Earth"

SageWoman: "Butterfly Woman"

San Pedro River Review: "The Pepper Tree," "Our Home"

Santa Fe Literary Review: "The Double"

Spillway: "Between Worlds," "Little Explosions"

The Americas Review: "Spells," "Ode to the Tortilla," "English con Salsa"

Third Wednesday: "Little Miracles," "Slowing"

Two Hawks Quarterly: "Origins"

University of Arizona Press: Infinite Divisions: "The Border"

University of California Press: Aztlán and Vietnam: "Heroes"

Voices of Mexico: "Rainbowoman"

We'Moon: "Those Birds"

Wising Up Press: The Kindness of Strangers: "Border Duende"

About the Author

Gina Valdés was born in Los Angeles and grew up on both sides of the United States-Mexico border. Poetry spellbound her at the age of six and the enchantment never left. She received degrees in Writing and Spanish Literature from the University of California, San Diego and has taught Literature and Writing at UCSD, UCDavis, UCLA, the University of Washington, and Colorado College. Her poetry has been widely published in the U.S., Mexico, and Europe, in five languages in nine countries. She resides in San Diego near family in the midst of abundant fauna and flora.

FLOWERSONG
P R E S S

FlowerSong Press nurtures essential verse from, about, and throughout the borderlands. Literary. Lyrical. Boundless.

Sign up for announcements about
new and upcoming titles at:

www.flowersongpress.com